SPOTLIGHT ON THE CIVIL RIGHTS MOVEMENT™

THE LIFE AND DEATH OF MALCOLM X

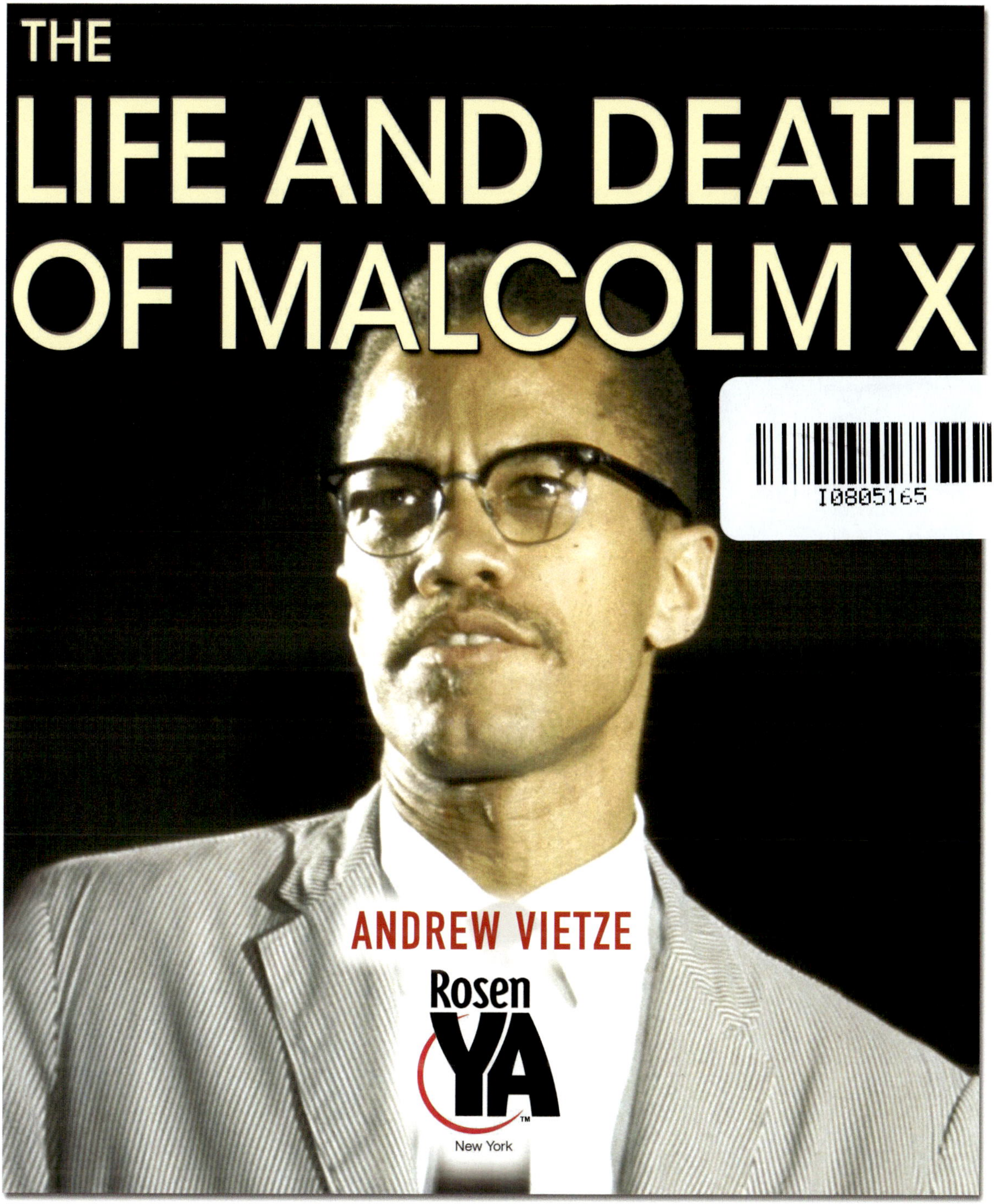

ANDREW VIETZE

Rosen YA™
New York

Published in 2018 by The Rosen Publishing Group, Inc.
29 East 21st Street, New York, NY 10010

First Edition

Library of Congress Cataloging-in-Publication Data

Names: Vietze, Andrew, author.
Title: The life and death of Malcolm X / Andrew Vietze.
Description: New York, NY : Rosen YA, 2018 | Series: Spotlight on the civil rights movement | Includes bibliographical references and index. | Audience: Grades 5–10.
Identifiers: LCCN 2017017631| ISBN 9781538380345 (library bound) | ISBN 9781538380314 (pbk.) | ISBN 9781538380321 (6 pack)
Subjects: LCSH: X, Malcolm, 1925–1965—Juvenile literature. | Black Muslims—Biography—Juvenile literature. | African American civil rights workers—Biography—Juvenile literature.
Classification: LCC E185.97.L5 V54 2018 | DDC 320.546092 [B]—dc23
LC record available at https://lccn.loc.gov/2017017631

Manufactured in the United States of America

On the cover: Iconic civil rights leader Malcolm X sent a message of defiance and anger to Americans who persisted in oppressing black Americans with unfair laws, practices, and beliefs.

CONTENTS

BLACK POWER!

In June 1964, black nationalist Malcolm X gave a speech in New York City. Famous worldwide, the radical leader announced the formation of the new Organization of Afro-American Unity, promising to bring blacks together to demand equality. His fiery, rousing speech focused on the treatment of blacks by whites. It was a big moment, summing up the career of one of the most in-demand speakers in the country. All across the United States, blacks, students, radicals, and others were marching in the streets, demanding social justice and equality for everyone—no matter the color of their skin. Most African Americans, like Dr. Martin Luther King Jr., wanted change to come peacefully. Malcolm X had other ideas. He told the audience that blacks would fight for their rights "by any means necessary." If that meant violence, they would meet violence with violence.

Malcolm X was a gifted orator who became nationally known for his powerful and inspiring speeches.

MALCOLM LITTLE

Malcolm X was born as Malcolm Little in Omaha, Nebraska, in 1925. When his mother was pregnant with him, she and his father were threatened by the local chapter of the Ku Klux Klan (KKK). Malcolm's father, Earl, was a local Baptist preacher and a member of the Universal Negro Improvement Association, a civil rights group. The KKK made several visits to the Little household in a pattern of harassment. The family moved to Wisconsin and later Michigan to escape but found things even worse. In Michigan, their home was burned to the ground. When Malcolm was six, Earl Little died on local train tracks. His death was ruled a suicide, but his family believed he

The KKK used intimidation and violence to harass Malcolm X's family, breaking the windows of their home with gun butts and threatening Malcolm's parents.

was killed by white supremacists because he stood up for blacks. Malcolm's mother had a hard time coping with her husband's death and was committed to a mental institution. Malcolm and his seven brothers and sisters were sent to foster homes.

LITTLE MALCOLM

A bright boy, Malcolm did well in school. The traumas of his childhood followed him, though, and he was a troubled youth. One of only a handful of black students at his Michigan high school, he was elected class president. He soon became discouraged, however. He told a teacher he wanted to become a lawyer, and the teacher told him that blacks didn't become lawyers. Seeing no future in school, he dropped out at fifteen years old and moved in with his sister in Boston, taking low-paying jobs. He fell in with the wrong crowd and turned to a life of crime. Because his hair had a red tinge, he became known in the criminal underworld as Detroit Red. He hung out in nightclubs wearing zoot suits and living large. In 1946, at the age of twenty, Malcolm Little was arrested for larceny and sentenced to ten years in prison.

As a young black man, Malcolm found little hope in school. Instead, he turned to the streets—and a life of petty crime.

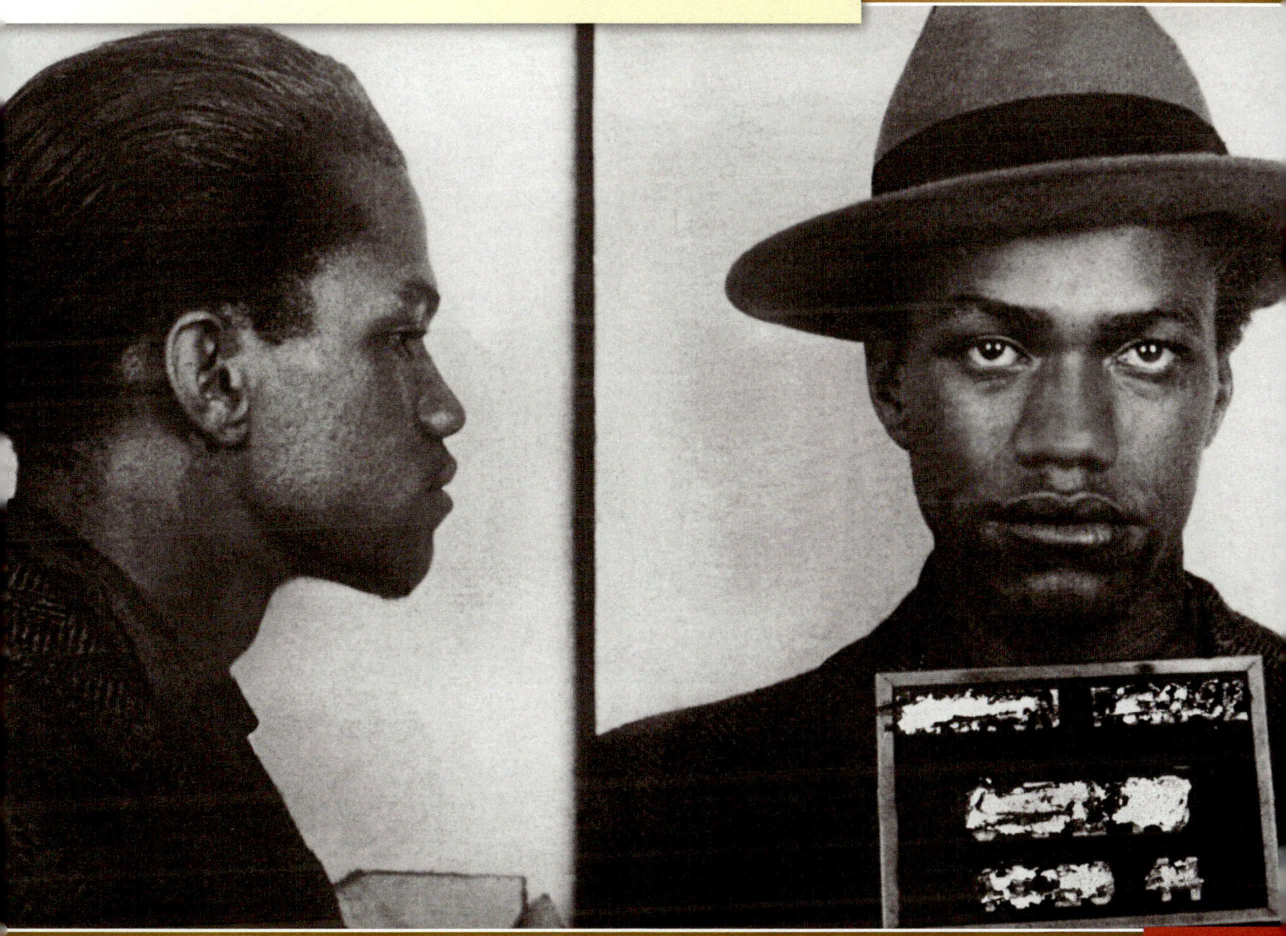

IN THE SLAMMER

Locked up in Charlestown State Prison, Malcolm Little befriended another inmate who suggested he sign up for a correspondence course. He did so. He took a class in grammar and penmanship, and then Latin. He read—a lot—ordering every book he could from the prison library. Because of good behavior and work on his behalf by his sister Ella, he was transferred to an experimental penitentiary, the Norfolk Prison Colony. This prison was luxurious compared to Charlestown. Malcolm had his own room and took classes taught by instructors from Harvard and other Boston-area universities. Norfolk had a far more extensive library, and Malcolm read widely. His brother Reginald came to visit and

Malcolm was an avid reader his entire life, and much of his time behind bars was spent educating himself.

told him about Allah and a religion made "for the black man." Reginald belonged to the Nation of Islam, which believed that blacks were the world's original people—and whites were the devil. Malcolm wanted in.

TRULY FREE

Every spare moment in prison, Malcolm Little had his head in a book. He read philosophy, literature, history, and a great deal about Muhammad and Islam. Reading not only occupied his mind, it also fed his soul and made his spirit soar. Before he knew it, he'd served his time. "Between Mr. Muhammad's teaching, my correspondence, my visitors—usually Ella and Reginald—and my reading of books," he says in his autobiography, "months passed without my even thinking about being imprisoned . . . In fact, up to then, I had never been so truly free in my life." He became a Muslim in prison and a staunch follower of the Nation of Islam. In 1952, Malcolm was released and moved in with his brother Wilfred in

In prison, Malcolm became a devoted follower of the black nationalist group Nation of Islam—and its charismatic leader, Elijah Muhammad.

Detroit. Later that year, Malcolm went with Wilfred and his family to see the head of the Nation of Islam, Elijah Muhammad, speak at a Muslim temple.

ENTER MUHAMMAD

Malcolm Little sat riveted while Elijah Muhammad spoke at the temple. Known as the Messenger, Muhammad wore a dark suit, white shirt, and bow tie. He told the audience that for centuries in North America the "blue-eyed devil white man" had brainwashed the "so-called Negro." The black man was the Original Man, he explained, kidnapped from his homeland and stripped of his culture by his oppressors. It was time for the black man to rise and take his rightful place again at the top of civilization. He then called out Malcolm Little's name, which felt like an electric jolt to the newly released man. Muhammad told the crowd how Little wrote to him almost every day in prison and was now at a crossroads. He could follow the devil and go back to his criminal ways or continue to be a good Muslim. Muhammad said he believed "he is going to remain faithful."

Malcolm led a clean-cut life upon his release from prison. His close-cut hair, glasses, and suit and tie became his signature look.

X FOR A NAME

After the speech, Elijah Muhammad asked Malcolm and his family to join him for dinner. There, Malcolm told Muhammad something that was bothering him at the temple he went to in Detroit. Not enough people were coming to the temple, not enough blacks were hearing what Muhammad was saying. Malcolm vowed to change that. He spent months working on recruiting members. Malcolm's efforts resulted in tripling the congregation's size, impressing Muhammad. He rose in prominence in the Nation of Islam, and he took a new name—Malcolm X. The X represented Malcolm's true, unknown African name. Malcolm wrote that it forever replaced the "white slavemaster name of 'Little.'" Malcolm X became an assistant minister, using oratory skills he learned in debate class in prison. Over the course of the next ten years, he worked his way up in the Nation of Islam organization and was placed in charge of his own temples in Harlem and Boston.

Malcolm quickly rose through the ranks of the Nation of Islam to became one of Elijah Muhammad's most important followers.

A GROWING NATION

In 1960, Malcolm X founded a national newspaper, *Muhammad Speaks*, spreading the message of the Nation of Islam. The organization was booming, growing from four hundred to forty thousand members, thanks in large part to Malcolm's hard work. America began to take notice of the Nation of Islam and its angry spokesman, Malcolm X. As the Nation of Islam grew, the movement for civil rights also budded across the country. Thousands of blacks boycotted the local bus service in Montgomery, Alabama, after a black woman, Rosa Parks, was fined for refusing to give her seat to a white man. The Civil Rights Act of 1957, a law that protected the rights of blacks to vote, passed in Congress. And the US Supreme Court decided that it was unconstitutional to force blacks and whites to go to separate schools. People were taking to the streets to fight for equality, and Malcolm X found ready crowds for his speeches.

The newspaper Malcolm X founded, *Muhammad Speaks*, was distributed in black neighborhoods. It attracted many followers to the Nation of Islam.

BETTY X

While he was building the Nation of Islam, Malcolm X fell in love with a young woman named Betty Sanders. A native of Detroit, Sanders had been an education major at the Tuskegee Institute in Alabama and later moved to New York. She worked in a local hospital, studying to be a nurse, and joined the Nation of Islam's Temple 7 in Harlem. In 1958, she became Betty X, Malcolm's wife. A strong, healthy home was important to Malcolm X. He and Betty had six daughters together. The first, Attallah, they named after Attila the Hun because Malcolm was impressed by the way he fought against the Roman Empire. Betty supported Malcolm's work, even though it took him away for much of the year. He said she gave him the foundation to do what he needed to build the Nation of Islam. He also said that she was the only woman he thought about loving.

Malcolm's wife, Betty Shabazz, became an inspirational figure herself, speaking at colleges and universities about civil rights.

BY ANY MEANS NECESSARY

Malcolm X began attracting large crowds by the force of his personality. He was a natural leader and a passionate speaker. As the civil rights movement was exploding all around the country, he found natural audiences for his speeches. His philosophy that the white man was the devil resonated with many. He pointed out how whites held blacks down by systematic oppression. How America called itself the land of the free and the home of the brave—but that was true only if you were white. He told blacks to rise up, with self-respect. He wanted them to build their own culture and communities. He said they should support their own people—and oppose integration with whites. Malcolm

By the late 1950s, Malcolm X became a famous figure, drawing huge crowds like the people shown here.

X's speeches were full of militant talk about "resistance" and "revolution." They should be ready, he said, to arm themselves and fight. They should take freedom "by any means necessary." Revolutions, he pointed out, always require bloodshed.

UNDER THE EYE OF THE FBI

Malcolm X's militant speeches caught the attention of those in power. By now a regular in newspapers and on TV, Malcolm X saw his profile rise even higher in 1959, when he was featured in a weeklong TV news program called *The Hate That Hate Produced.* With his trademark brow-line eye-glasses, dark suit, and white shirt, he was recognized everywhere he went. Among those keeping a keen eye on Malcolm was the Federal Bureau of Investigation (FBI), which began watching him as soon as he was released from prison. The FBI eventually amassed a whole filing case of information on "Malcolm Little," totaling more than 3,500 pages of documents. This was not surprising since the black leader met with Cuban communist Fidel Castro and preached black nationalism. He said that the United

Malcolm X believed strongly in revolution and met with Cuban communist leader Fidel Castro, among other world leaders.

States' capitalist system was built on racism and told blacks to arm themselves. The FBI kept files on many famous people of the time, from John Lennon of the Beatles to writers Norman Mailer and Truman Capote to boxer Muhammad Ali.

MALCOLM X VS. DR. KING

As the fight for civil rights unfolded, Americans were divided. Many thought everyone should be equal, no matter the color of their skin. Others believed whites were superior to blacks and thought that laws shouldn't be changed to make things fair. The black community was divided, too. On one side were the supporters of Malcolm X and the Nation of Islam. They argued that blacks should be equal to and separate from whites. On the other side were the followers of Dr. Martin Luther King Jr., who believed in using nonviolent means as a force for change. Malcolm X thought King and his followers were naïve and would never get anywhere preaching peace and refusing to fight back.

Martin Luther King Jr. gave his iconic "I Have a Dream" speech at the famous March on Washington. Malcolm X was not impressed, calling it a "picnic" rather than the angry demonstration he felt it should have been.

He called King's massive rally, the March on Washington, where King made his famous "I Have a Dream" speech, the "Farce on Washington." King said, "I feel that Malcolm has done himself and our people a great disservice."

LEAVING THE NATION

In 1962, Malcolm X discovered that Elijah Muhammad was not the man he had thought he was. The Messenger set very high standards of conduct for members of the Nation of Islam. But he didn't meet them himself. Muhammad had fathered several children with women other than his wife. Malcolm expressed his disappointment, and the two had a disagreement. Things got worse when Muhammad criticized Malcolm X for some comments he made about the assassination of President John F. Kennedy. Malcolm X had said that the president had made promises to blacks that he didn't keep and that he never "foresaw that the chickens would come home to roost so soon."

Malcolm X felt that President John F. Kennedy was killed by the same hate that whites were spreading toward blacks.

In other words, he got what he deserved. Muhammad found the statement offensive and suspended Malcolm X from representing the Nation of Islam. Malcolm thought it was now time to form a new organization.

MALCOLM IN MECCA

Malcolm decided to take some time off and traveled to Europe, Africa, and the Middle East. He marveled at the kindness of strangers—both black and white. When he visited Islam's most holy place, Mecca, he found it didn't matter that he was black or that he was famous. He was the same as every other pilgrim. He met Muslims from China, Russia, Japan, Indonesia, Afghanistan, and Ghana, all there for the same reason. One of the people who helped him the most "would have been called a white man in America." Malcolm was amazed. "[I]t struck me hard and instantly," he said in his autobiography. "I had no feeling of him being a white man . . ." The man was warm and kind and treated Malcolm like a brother. "I was speechless at the man's attitude, and at my own physical feeling of no difference between us as human beings."

Malcolm's pilgrimage to the Muslim holy city of Mecca, in Saudia Arabia, made him rethink his life.

SHABAZZ

Malcolm X's trip to Mecca changed him profoundly. He converted to traditional Islam, which was very different than the Nation of Islam's version, and changed his name to el-Hajj Malik el-Shabazz. He became less militant—and more full of hope and optimism. He began to see the battle for civil rights as something more than just a fight with the white man. When he was in Saudi Arabia, he felt a brotherhood with all his fellow Muslims that transcended race. It was an experience that he had previously felt "never could exist between the white and the non-white." He began to see the institutionalized racism of America in a different light, as a struggle against global economic and political forces. Malcolm

Malcolm's distrust of white people softened when he met white Muslim brothers and sisters in Saudi Arabia.

began to pour his energy into the political party he formed as an alternative to the Nation of Islam. He called it the Organization of Afro-American Unity (OAAU).

VIOLENCE IN THE STREETS

Just like the militant Nation of Islam, the OAAU would arm itself and fight back if need be. Malcolm said in a speech, "Be nonviolent only with those who are nonviolent to you." Violence was spreading across the South, where blacks were being lynched by racist mobs. Black churches were bombed, huge riots broke out, and buses carrying Freedom Rider civil rights activists were attacked and burned. National Guard troops were mobilized to restore order. Malcolm X didn't think they were doing a good enough job and said the OAAU would send its own troops if need be. "If you have a rifle, I must have a rifle. If you have a club, I must have a club.

Malcolm X didn't believe National Guard troops could—or would—protect protesters during the chaotic 1960s. He said his fellow blacks should arm themselves for the fight.

This is equality." At the end of his speech, he called for cooperation with the Nation of Islam. He told Elijah Muhammad they should fight their enemies—not each other.

MALCOLM X WILL DIE

Many members of the Nation of Islam saw Malcolm X's new organization as a threat. Some were bothered that he had softened—even slightly—in his stance on race relations. He had begun to think that maybe the country could heal itself and bring about equality through understanding rather than violence. Malcolm X's approach was attracting many new followers, and the Nation of Islam didn't like it. The FBI learned about potential attempts on his life. One undercover operative said he was ordered to place a bomb in Malcolm X's car by Nation of Islam authorities. Talk between the two organizations was often heated. Malcolm X began to take bodyguards with him everywhere he went. One night in

Malcolm X's home in Elmhurst, New York, was firebombed. In front of the house sits furniture damaged in the firebombing.

February 1965, four Molotov cocktails were thrown through the windows of his home. Luckily, no one was injured. Betty Shabazz said they received an anonymous phone call one night: "better wake up before it's too late."

ASSASSINATION!

On February 21, 1965, Malcolm X stepped up to the podium to address a meeting of the OAAU in Harlem. He offered a greeting. A hubbub arose in the audience. He raised his hands to quiet the crowd and shots rang out. Malcolm fell onto the stage. Two men were tackled by audience members and held until police arrived. A third fled. Malcolm X was rushed to Columbia Presbyterian Medical Center, where he was pronounced dead. He was thirty-nine. All three men, members of the Nation of Islam, were apprehended. They were all sentenced to prison for murder.

The death of Malcolm X was felt all across America. Many commented on how he was struck down just as he was moving away from violence. Malcolm had begun working on an autobiography with writer Arthur Haley. *The Autobiography of Malcolm X* sold millions of copies and broadcast the civil rights leader's message further than ever before.

★ DAILY NEWS 10¢

NEW YORK'S PICTURE NEWSPAPER ®

Vol. 46. No. 207 Copr. 1965 News Syndicate Co. Inc. New York, N.Y. 10017, Monday, February 22, 1965★ WEATHER: Partly cloudy, cold, windy.

MALCOLM X MURDERED

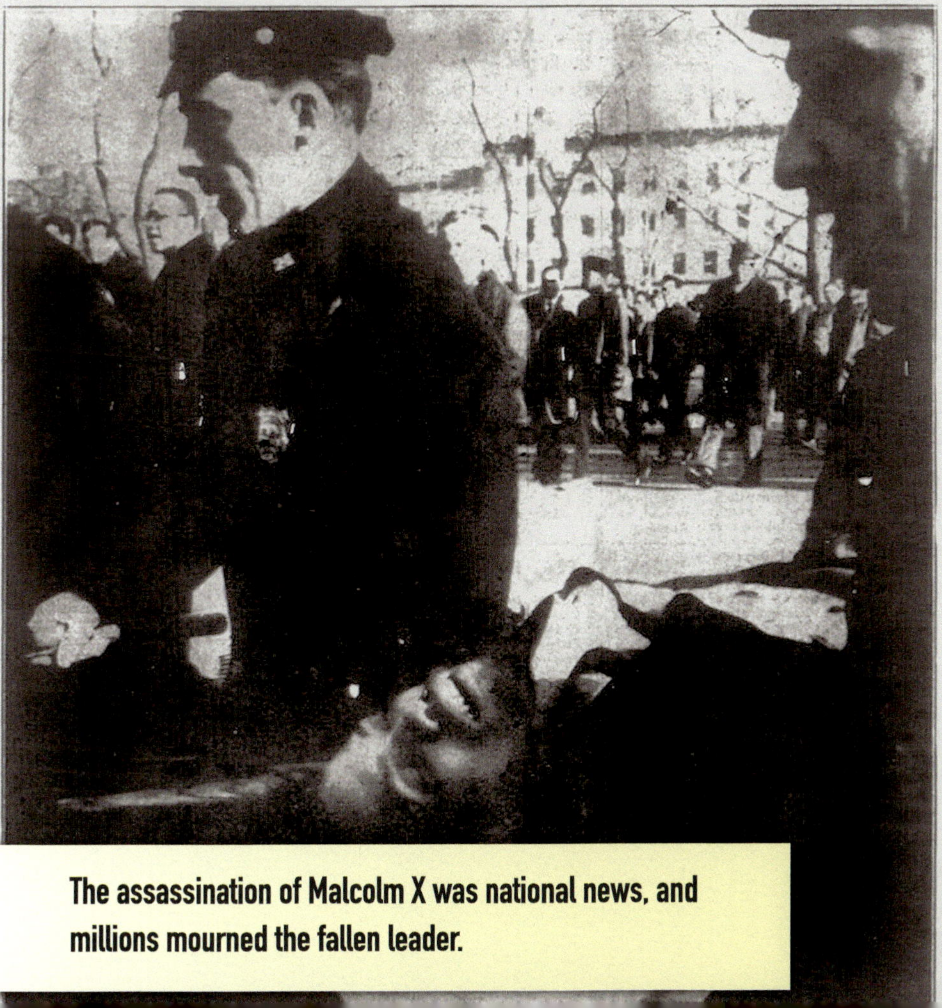

Gunned Down at Rally

Malcolm X, 39, is carried from Audubon Ballroom, 166th St. and Broadway, after he was shot while addressing a rally of his followers yesterday afternoon. He was declared dead at the Vanderbilt Clinic of Columbia-Presbyterian Medical Center within 15 minutes of the attack. Two men were taken by force from a howling mob of Malcolm's followers who were pummeling them on the street after the assassination. The slim Negro leader had been charging the Black Muslims with plotting to kill him ever since he defected from the year ag

Story on p

The assassination of Malcolm X was national news, and millions mourned the fallen leader.

LEGACY OF A LEADER

Thanks to the publication of his autobiography, millions began to see Malcolm X in a new light. Readers saw him as more than just a militant black man. He was an advocate for radical change, but he was also a man who grew and changed after a childhood of trauma and violence. They saw that in many ways, his was a quintessentially American story—he pulled himself up through self-education and hard work to become famous and influential. He showed generations of young blacks they could do the same and that they should be proud of their heritage. Through his speeches—and, even more, through his writing—Malcolm X held up a mirror

Malcolm X's legacy lives on in continuing sales of his autobiography and honors like city streets being named after him.

to the nation, showing how badly blacks had been mistreated. He inspired generations of blacks to stand up for themselves, and in so doing became one of the most important African Americans in the history of the United States.

GLOSSARY

autobiography The life story of a person as told by himself or herself.

boycott To refuse to deal with a business or group because of their actions.

brainwash To persuade a person to adopt a viewpoint through the use of propaganda.

conduct A type of behavior.

correspondence course A course of study carried on by mail.

institutionalize To create a structured, formal system.

integrate To blend together.

lynch To kill a person by a mob, usually by hanging.

militant Aggressive.

Molotov cocktail A homemade bomb using a bottle.

oratory The art of effective and influential public speaking.

pilgrim One who travels to a holy place as a worshipper.

quintessential The most typical example of a thing or time.

radical Political views that are very different from the views of most of society.

systematic oppression The government's use of laws and police to support a system of inferiority and superiority among people.

transcend To go beyond.

unconstitutional Not according to the law of the land.

zoot suit A style of men's suits in the 1940s with long loose jackets, padded shoulders, and tapered trousers with high waists.

Canadian Museum for Human Rights
85 Israel Asper Way
Winnipeg, MB R3C 0L5
Canada
(204) 289-2000
Website: https://humanrights.ca
Facebook: @canadianmuseumforhumanrights
Twitter: @CMHR_News
Instagram: @cmhr_mcdp
This museum showcases the human rights history of the United States' northern neighbor.

Malcolm X and Dr. Betty Shabazz Memorial and Educational Center
3940 Broadway
New York, NY 10032
(212) 568-1341
Website: http://www.theshabazzcenter.net
Facebook: @theshabazzcenter
Twitter: @shabazzcenter
A museum dedicated to the life of Malcolm X and his wife, Dr. Betty Shabazz, the Shabazz Center features videos, writings, and displays.

Malcolm X Birth Site
3448 Evans Street
Omaha, NE 68111
(402) 881-8118
Website: http://www.malcolmxfoundation.org
The Malcolm X Foundation, with the help of some Shabazz family members, hosts a tribute to the great leader at the site of his birth in Omaha.

National Civil Rights Museum
450 Mulberry Street
Memphis, TN 38103
(901) 521-9699
Website: http://www.civilrightsmuseum.org
Facebook: @NCRMuseum
Twitter: @NCRMuseum
Instagram: @ncrmuseum
Affiliated with the Smithsonian Institution, the National Civil Rights Museum explores the history of the civil rights movement and its important role in the story of the United States.

National Museum of African American History and Culture
1400 Constitution Avenue NW
Washington, DC 20560
(844) 750-3012
Website: https://nmaahc.si.edu
Facebook: @NMAAHC
Twitter: @nmaahc
Instagram: @nmaahc
Run by the Smithsonian Institution, this is the only national museum devoted to the African American experience.

WEBSITES

Because of the changing nature of internet links, Rosen Publishing has developed an online list of websites related to the subject of this book. This site is updated regularly. Please use this link to access this list:

http://www.rosenlinks.com/SCRM/MalcolmX

FOR FURTHER READING

Aretha, David. *Time for Martyrs: The Life of Malcolm X*. Greensboro, NC: Morgan Reynolds Publications, 2012.

Burlingame, Jeff. *Malcolm X: I Believe in the Brotherhood of Men, All Men*. New York, NY: Enslow Publishers, 2010.

Doeden, Matt. *A Marked Man: The Assassination of Malcolm X*. Minneapolis, MN: Twenty-First Century Books, 2013.

Draper, Alison Stark. *The Assassination of Malcolm X*. New York, NY: Rosen Publishing, 2002.

Gundersen, Jessica, and Seitu Hayden. *X: A Biography of Malcolm X*. North Mankato, MN: Capstone Press, 2011.

Helfer, Andrew, and Randy DuBurke. *Malcolm X: A Graphic Biography*. New York, NY: Hill and Wang, 2006.

Jeffrey, Laura S. *Betty Shabazz: Sharing the Vision of Malcolm X*. New York, NY: Enslow Publishers, 2000.

Meyers, Walter Dean. *Malcolm X: By Any Means Necessary*. New York, NY: Scholastic, 1994.

Shabazz, Ilyasah, and Kekla Magoon. *X*. Somerville, MA: Candlewick Press, 2015.

BIBLIOGRAPHY

Ali, Zaheer. "What Really Happened to Malcolm X." CNN, February 17, 2015. http://www.cnn.com/2015/02/17/opinion/ali-malcolm-x-assassination-anniversary.

Coates, Ta-Nehisi. "The Legacy of Malcolm X." *The Atlantic,* May 2011.

International Herald Tribune. "1965: Malcolm X Dies: Shot 4 Times at New York Rally." *New York Herald Tribune*, February 22, 1965. https://iht-retrospective.blogs.nytimes.com/2015/02/23/1965-malcolm-x-dies-shot-4-times-at-new-york-rally/?rref=collection%2Ftimestopic%2FMalcolm%20X.

International Herald Tribune. "1966: Verdict in Malcolm X's Killing." *New York Herald Tribune*, March 12, 1966. https://iht-retrospective.blogs.nytimes.com/2016/03/11/1966-verdict-in-malcolm-xs-killing/?rref=collection%2Ftimestopic%2FMalcolm%20X&_r=0.

Kihss, Peter. "Malcolm X Shot to Death at Rally Here." *New York Times*, February 22, 1965.

New York Times. "Malcolm X Letters Show His Evolution." March 8, 2002. http://www.nytimes.com/2002/03/08/us/malcolm-x-letters-show-his-evolution.html.

World History Project. "Malcolm X Timeline." https://worldhistoryproject.org/topics/malcolm-x.

X, Malcolm. *The Autobiography of Malcolm X.* New York, NY: Ballantine Books, 2015.

X, Malcolm. "The Ballot or the Bullet." Speech delivered in Cleveland, OH, at a meeting sponsored by the local chapter of the Congress on Racial Equality, April 3, 1964. http://www.edchange.org/multicultural/speeches/malcolm_x_ballot.html.

INDEX

About the Author

Andrew Vietze is the best-selling author of several biographies about American heroes, including Rosen's Spotlight on the Civil Rights Movement title *The Life and Death of Martin Luther King Jr.* His work has been featured on the Travel Channel and won multiple awards. *The Autobiography of Malcolm X* was one of his favorite books as a kid. Find out more at www.andrewvietze.com.

Photo Credits

Cover, p. 1 Robert Parent/The LIFE Images Collection/Getty Images; pp. 3, 42, 43, 45, 46, 47 Onur Ersin/Shutterstock.com; pp. 4, 6, 8, 10, 12, 14, 16, 18, 20, 22, 24, 26, 28, 30, 32, 34, 36, 38, 40 Sergey Kamshylin/Shutterstock.com; pp. 5, 9, 13, 19, 21, 23, 37 Bettmann /Getty Images; p. 7 herlordship/iStock/Thinkstock; p. 11 Baloncici /Shutterstock.com; p. 15 Afro Newspaper/Gado/Archive Photos/Getty Images; p. 17 Frank Scherschel/The LIFE Picture Collection/Getty Images; p. 25 © AP Images; p. 27 Francis Miller/The LIFE Picture Collection/Getty Images; p. 29 Wally McNamee/Corbis Historical /Getty Images; p. 31 miravisoko/Shutterstock.com; p. 33 Pictorial Parade/Archive Photos/Getty Images; p. 35 Lee Lockwood/The LIFE Images Collection/Getty Images; p. 39 New York Daily News Archive /New York Daily News/Getty Images; p. 41 Osugi/Shutterstock.com.

Designer: Nelson Sá; Editor and Photo Researcher: Xina M. Uhl